# More Than Enough

*Discovering God's Radical Provision When You Can't See a Way Forward*

J. Randolph Turpin, Jr.

# More Than Enough

*Discovering God's Radical Provision When You Can't See a Way Forward*

J. Randolph Turpin, Jr.

DECLARATION PRESS

**More Than Enough: Discovering God's Radical Provision When You Can't See a Way Forward**



Published by Declaration Press in the United States of America



ISBN: 979-8-9891257-5-3

*For everyone who has ever sat at a kitchen table*

*staring at bills they couldn't pay,*

*wondering if it would ever get better.*

*God is not finished with your story.*

# Contents

INTRODUCTION

# The God Who Sees You

You didn't pick up this book by accident.

Maybe someone handed it to you. Maybe you found it on a shelf or stumbled across it in an online store. However it arrived in your hands, I believe something bigger than coincidence is at work here. There is a God in heaven who sees exactly where you are right now — the worry behind your eyes, the weight on your chest, the numbers that don't add up, the quiet fear you carry into every new month — and He has something to say to you.

What He wants to say is this: I am not finished with you.

This book is not a financial planning guide. You won't find budgeting worksheets or debt payoff strategies in these pages. There are good books for that, and perhaps one day you'll read them. But this is not that book.

This book is for your soul.

It is for the part of you that has started to believe that this is just how your life is — that lack is your permanent address, that struggle is your identity, that other people get breakthroughs but you are somehow exempt from God's goodness. It is for the wounded places in you that have quietly given up hope.

I have written this book because I want you to know something: the most important shift that needs to happen in your life right now is not in your bank account. It is in your beliefs.

Can positive thinking magically fix your bills? No. It can't. But what you believe about God, about yourself, and about your future *can* create the culture you live in — and the culture you live in shapes everything else.

You can move from a culture of lack to a culture of abundance. Not overnight. Not without process. But it is absolutely, gloriously possible.

And it starts here. It starts with what you believe.

So settle in. God has a word for you. And I have a hunch that by the time you finish this book, something will have shifted — not just in your thinking, but in the very atmosphere of your life.

Let's begin.

CHAPTER ONE

# You Are Not What Your Balance Says

> *"For I know the plans I have for you, declares the LORD, plans to prosper you and not to harm you, plans to give you hope and a future."* — **Jeremiah 29:11**

Let me start by saying something that I hope lands in the deepest part of you:

Your bank account balance is not your identity.

I know that sounds simple. Maybe even obvious. But the truth is, when you are living under the daily pressure of financial lack, it becomes almost impossible not to let those numbers define you. When you check your balance, and it says there's not enough, something in you starts to agree, saying that *you* are not enough.

That is a lie. And we need to clearly identify and define that lie before we go any further.

## The Story You've Been Told

Somewhere along the way — maybe in childhood, maybe in a season of failure, maybe slowly and almost imperceptibly over years of struggle — you absorbed a story. It goes something like this:

"People like me don't get ahead. I come from a family that always struggled. I've never been good with money. Every time I get a little ahead, something knocks me back down. God blesses other people, but I'm somehow always on the outside looking in."

Does any of that sound familiar?

That story is the enemy's greatest weapon against your financial future. Not your debt. Not your income level. Not your lack of education or your past mistakes. The story is the problem, because as long as you believe that story, you will unconsciously make decisions, speak words, and adopt postures that confirm it. You will live into it.

The good news — the staggering, almost-too-good-to-be-true news — is that God has a completely different story in mind for you. And His story has been there from the beginning.

## How God Sees You

> *"Before I formed you in the womb I knew you, before you were born I set you apart."* — **Jeremiah 1:5**

God does not see you as a person defined by lack. He does not look at your overdrawn account and sigh with disappointment. He does not see a failure when He looks at you. He sees someone He formed intentionally, someone He knows completely, someone He has called and equipped, and someone He has planned for. That's what Jeremiah 29:11 suggests.

Now, scholars rightly note that Jeremiah wrote those words— *"I know the plans I have for you"* — to a nation in Babylonian exile, not as a personal promise to every reader who underlines them. Fair enough. But theology works by revealing who God is — and a God who speaks shalom over an entire displaced people, in their darkest corporate moment, is the same God who meets you at your kitchen table. His nature doesn't change with the audience.

The word "prosper" in Jeremiah 29:11 comes from the Hebrew word *shalom* — a word so rich it barely fits in any single English translation. It means wholeness. Completeness. Nothing missing, nothing broken. Flourishing in every dimension of life.

That is God's plan for you. Not barely surviving. Not white-knuckling it through every month. Shalom.

You may be in a season that does not look anything like shalom right now. I understand that. But a season is not a life sentence. And a current condition is not a permanent identity.

## The Difference Between a Season and an Identity

This is one of the most important distinctions I can offer you: there is a massive difference between going through a hard season and being a hard-luck person.

Seasons change. Identities stick — unless we deliberately choose different ones.

The Bible is full of people who went through devastating financial and circumstantial hardship. Job lost everything in a single day. Ruth was a widowed immigrant with no visible means of support. David spent years living in caves and running for his life. Joseph was sold into slavery by his own brothers and then thrown into prison on false charges.

Not one of those people was defined by their season. And in every case, God's plan was bigger than the hardship.

Job's latter days were greater than his former. Ruth became the great-grandmother of King David. David became the most celebrated king in Israel's history. Joseph became the second most powerful man in the ancient world — and used that power to save millions of lives, including the very brothers who had sold him.

Their circumstances were not their identity. And neither are yours.

## A New Introduction

I want to invite you to try something. Instead of introducing yourself (even internally) as someone who struggles financially, as someone who can never catch a break, as someone stuck in cycles of poverty — what if you started to practice a new introduction?

Something like this:

*I am a child of the God who owns everything. I am deeply loved by the God who plans to prosper me. I am in a hard season, but I am not a hard-luck person. My latter days are going to be greater than my former days. God is not finished with my story.*

You may not fully believe that yet. That's okay. Faith often begins as a choice before it becomes a feeling. Speak it anyway. Your words are seeds, and seeds take time to grow.

But they always grow.

## DECLARATIONS

- **I am not defined by my bank account. I am defined by *whose* I am.**
- **I am a child of the God who owns the cattle on a thousand hills.**
- **My current season is not my permanent identity.**
- **God has plans for me — plans for shalom, for wholeness, for nothing missing.**
- **I refuse to let a number on a computer screen tell me who I am.**
- **My latter days will be greater than my former days.**

CHAPTER TWO

# Jehovah Jireh: The Lord Who Provides

*"Abraham looked up and there in a thicket he saw a ram caught by its horns. He went over and took the ram and sacrificed it as a burnt offering instead of his son. So Abraham called that place The LORD Will Provide."*
**— Genesis 22:13–14**

There is a name of God that I want to plant deep in your heart in this chapter, because it is a name that was born in one of the most desperate moments in all of human history.

Jehovah Jireh.

The Lord Will Provide.

Abraham coined this name at the very moment when his situation seemed most impossible. He had climbed a mountain prepared to give up the most precious thing he had ever been given. He was at the end of his own ability to solve the problem. And it was exactly then — at the end of himself — that God showed up with provision that Abraham could not have seen from the valley.

There is something profoundly important in that story for you today.

## He Sees What You Cannot

The name Jireh comes from a Hebrew word meaning "to see." Jehovah Jireh literally means "the LORD who sees ahead" — or even more beautifully, "the LORD who sees to it."

God is not scrambling to figure out how to help you. He is not watching your situation with concern, wondering if things will work out. He is already in your tomorrow, and He has already seen the provision. He sees what you cannot see from the valley you are standing in.

From where you are, all you can see is the mountain. God sees the other side.

From where you are, all you can see is the empty bank account. God sees the ram in the thicket.

From where you are, all you can see is the problem. God sees — and has already arranged — the provision.

> *"And my God will meet all your needs according to the riches of his glory in Christ Jesus."* — **Philippians 4:19**

Paul did not write that God *might* meet your needs, or that God will *try* to meet your needs, or that God will meet your needs if you do everything right. He wrote that God *will* meet all your needs — and that the source from which He draws is not the economy of your nation, not the goodwill of your employer, not the fluctuating price of goods. It is the riches of His glory.

Let that sink in. The riches of His glory. That is a supply line that does not run out.

## God Has Always Been a Provider

This is not a New Testament development. The thread of God's provision runs through every book of the Bible like a golden cord.

He provided for Adam and Eve — not just food and shelter, but relationship, purpose, and belonging. Even after the Fall, He clothed them. He did not abandon them.

He provided manna and quail and water from a rock for an entire nation wandering in a desert for forty years. Think about the logistics of that. Millions of people. No agriculture. No market.

No infrastructure. Just the wild provision of a God who sees and who acts.

He provided for Elijah through a widow who herself had only enough for a final meal. He provided for that same widow for years — her jar of flour never running out, her jug of oil never going dry. A supernatural economy operating inside a household that, by natural standards, had nothing.

He provided for Daniel in a pagan empire, for Joseph in a foreign prison, for Ruth in a stranger's field.

And He will provide for you.

## Provision Is Part of His Character

I want you to understand something crucial: God's provision is not just something He does. It is part of who He is.

Jehovah Jireh is His name. Not His job title. His name.

When God introduces Himself as Provider, He is telling you something permanent and unalterable about His nature. He cannot fail to provide any more than the sun can fail to give light. It is what He is.

This means that when you are in lack, something in the very heart of God is moved toward you. You are not irritating Him. You are not exhausting His patience. You are not too broken or too far gone or too much of a slow learner.

You are precisely the kind of person Jehovah Jireh came for.

## The Ram Was Already There

Here is a thought worth considering about the story in Genesis 22: the ram was likely already in the thicket when Abraham was still climbing the mountain.

God did not scramble at the last second. The provision was already in place before the moment of need arrived.

Whatever you are facing right now — whatever bill is coming due, whatever need is pressing in, whatever gap exists between what you have and what you need — I want you to know that God is not in a panic. The ram is already in the thicket. The provision already exists. You simply haven't seen it yet.

Lift your eyes. The provision is closer than it looks.

# DECLARATIONS

• My God is Jehovah Jireh — the God who sees ahead and who provides.

• He will meet all my needs according to the riches of His glory.

• The provision already exists. I just haven't seen it yet.

• God is not scrambling. He has already arranged for my breakthrough.

• His supply line is the riches of His glory — it does not run out.

• I am not too far gone for God's provision to reach me.

CHAPTER THREE

# The Mindset That Changes Everything

> *"Do not conform to the pattern of this world, but be transformed by the renewing of your mind. Then you will be able to test and approve what God's will is — his good, pleasing and perfect will."* — **Romans 12:2**

If I could hand you one key for the journey from lack to abundance, it would be this: your mindset is your most important asset.

Not your income. Not your education. Not your opportunities. Not even, as we explored in the last chapter, your current circumstances. Your mindset.

This is not pop psychology. This is biblical theology. Paul's instruction to be "transformed by the renewing of your mind" may be one of the most radical statements in the New Testament — because it implies that transformation is possible, that it is accessible to ordinary people, and that it begins in the invisible realm of thought before it ever shows up in the visible realm of circumstance.

Transformation comes through renewed thinking. Changed thinking. Restructured, reoriented, Spirit-empowered thinking.

## Two Economies

There are two economies operating in the world simultaneously. One is the economy of scarcity — the visible, natural system that says resources are limited, opportunities are finite, and what you have is what you've got. The other is the economy of the Kingdom — the invisible, supernatural system that operates by entirely different rules.

The economy of scarcity says: There is not enough.

The Kingdom economy says: My God shall supply all your need.

The economy of scarcity says: The rich get richer and the poor get poorer.

The Kingdom economy says: The blessing of the Lord makes rich, and He adds no sorrow to it.

The economy of scarcity says: Your past determines your future.

The Kingdom economy says: Behold, I am doing a new thing.

A poverty mindset is simply the habit of thinking exclusively from the economy of scarcity while ignoring the economy of the Kingdom. It is not a character flaw. It is not a sin. It is a learned pattern of thought — which means it can be unlearned, and a new pattern can take its place.

## What a Poverty Mindset Sounds Like

Before we can replace a mindset, we need to recognize it. Here are some of the most common thought patterns of a scarcity mindset. As you read them, notice how familiar and how normal they might feel:

*"There's never enough."*

*"Every time I get ahead, something happens to knock me back."*

*"I don't deserve good things."*

*"Money is the root of all evil — wanting more is greedy."*

*"Rich people are corrupt. Wealth is bad."*

*"I'll believe it when I see it."*

*"God blesses other people — I'm just not that lucky."*

*"I'm just not a money person."*

*"Why bother trying? It never works out anyway."*

Any of those ring a bell? Most people wrestling with financial hardship will recognize several of them. Some people will recognize all of them.

Here is what I need you to understand: these are not just negative thoughts. They are beliefs. And beliefs have power. What you believe, you will tend to act on. What you act on shapes your decisions. Your decisions shape your life.

The good news is that these are *not facts*. They are *stories*. And stories can be rewritten.

## What an Abundance Mindset Sounds Like

An abundance mindset is not wishful thinking or denial of reality. It is the courageous choice to think in alignment with what God has said, even when circumstances say otherwise.

An abundance mindset sounds like this:

*"God is my source. Every channel may dry up, but the Source never does."*

*"I am a generous person. Generosity flows naturally from me."*

*"Good things are in my future. God has plans to prosper me."*

*"I am learning. I am growing. This season is making me wiser."*

*"Wealth is a tool, and I will use it well when it comes."*

*"I am a steward of God's resources. I manage them with wisdom and faith."*

*"Breakthrough is normal for people who belong to Jehovah Jireh."*

Notice that these are not statements about your current situation. They are statements about your identity and your trajectory. They are declarations of who you are becoming, not just a description of where you are.

And this is how mindset change works: you speak who you are becoming before you fully arrive there. You practice the new story until it becomes more real to you than the old one.

## The Renewal Process

Paul says we are transformed by the renewing of our minds. The word "renewing" in the Greek is a compound word that means a complete, thorough renovation. Not a fresh coat of paint. A complete overhaul.

This is not a quick fix. It is a process. But it is a process that works — and every step of it is available to you right now, in your current circumstances, without waiting for your finances to change first.

Here is the simple process: identify the limiting belief, reject it as a lie, find what God's Word says instead, and deliberately practice the new belief through declaration and repetition until it becomes your natural way of thinking.

This is precisely what we will be doing throughout the rest of this book.

One renewed thought at a time. One declaration at a time. One choice at a time.

This is how people change. This is how cultures change. This is how you change.

## DECLARATIONS

- **My mindset is my most important asset, and I am actively renewing it.**
- **I choose to think from the economy of the Kingdom, not the economy of scarcity.**
- **What God has said about me is more true than what my circumstances say.**

• I am not a victim of my past thinking. I am choosing new thoughts today.

• Transformation is possible for me because God's Word says so.

• Breakthrough is normal for someone who belongs to Jehovah Jireh.

CHAPTER FOUR

# Gratitude: Your Most Underestimated Weapon

> *"Give thanks in all circumstances; for this is God's will for you in Christ Jesus."* — **1 Thessalonians 5:18**

I want to talk to you about one of the most powerful forces available to human beings — and one of the most neglected by people in financial difficulty.

Gratitude.

Now, I know what you might be thinking. How am I supposed to be grateful when I can't pay my bills? What exactly am I supposed to be thankful for when the electricity might get shut off, and I'm eating ramen for the third week in a row?

Let's address this honestly.

Paul did not say to be thankful *for* all circumstances. He said to give thanks *in* all circumstances. There is a crucial difference. He is not asking you to be glad that you're struggling. But he *is* inviting you to cultivate the discipline of finding something to be grateful for even in the midst of the struggle.

And when you do — when you genuinely practice this — something remarkable happens.

## What Gratitude Does to Your Brain and Soul

Gratitude is not just a spiritual discipline. It is a restructuring agent. When you practice genuine thankfulness, it literally redirects your attention. And what you give your attention to grows.

A *scarcity mindset* is, at its core, a relentless focus on what you lack. *Gratitude* is the intentional, deliberate practice of focusing on what you have. When you shift your focus from lack to gift — even small gifts, even simple ones — you begin to see your life differently.

And here is the theological backbone of this: every good gift and every perfect gift comes from the Father of lights. That means that every single thing you have that is good — your breath, your sight, the roof over your head, the people who love you, the coffee in your cup, the sunrise this morning — is evidence of a God who is providing for you right now.

Gratitude trains your eyes to see the provision that is already present.

## Ten Thousand Gifts

The writer of Psalm 103 is one of the great practitioners of intentional gratitude in all of Scripture. Listen to how he begins:

> *"Praise the LORD, my soul; all my inmost being, praise his holy name. Praise the LORD, my soul, and forget not all his benefits."* — **Psalm 103:1–2**

Forget not all his benefits. This implies that forgetting is a real danger — and a common one. In the press of daily hardship, it is staggeringly easy to forget what God has already done. The psalmist is essentially preaching to himself: Pay attention. Count the gifts. Do not let the noise of lack drown out the testimony of grace.

He goes on to list specifics: God forgives all your sins. God heals all your diseases. God redeems your life from the pit. God crowns you with love and compassion. God satisfies your desires with good things.

This is the testimony of a man who has known hardship — and who has chosen, in the middle of it, to keep his eyes on the goodness of God.

## The Testimony Loop

There is something that happens in the human soul when you recall and declare what God has already done: faith rises.

This is why testimony is so powerful. When you speak out loud — even to yourself, even in the quiet of your car or your bedroom — "God came through for me before. He will come through for me again" — something shifts. Courage appears where fear was living. Hope displaces despair. The story of your life starts to change.

I want to encourage you to start a gratitude practice that is specific, not generic. It is easy to say "I'm thankful for my family and my health" in a routine, half-hearted way that doesn't actually move anything. I'm inviting you to go deeper.

What specific thing did God do for you last week? What prayer did He answer — even partially? What need got met in an unexpected way? Who showed up in your life with exactly what you needed? Where did you see provision you hadn't anticipated?

Start writing these things down. Build a record. You are creating evidence — a body of testimony that says: this God provides. This God shows up. This God is faithful even when circumstances are hard.

That record will carry you through the moments when you cannot feel it. The testimony of what God has done is the foundation of confidence in what He will do.

## Gratitude Is an Act of Warfare

In 2 Chronicles 20, King Jehoshaphat faced an enemy army so vast and so overwhelming that, by every natural calculation, he had already lost. His response is one of the most remarkable strategies in military history: he sent the worship team out in front of the army.

Gratitude and praise were his weapons. And the enemy was defeated before a single sword was drawn.

I am not suggesting that if you just feel thankful enough, your financial situation will magically resolve. But I am saying that gratitude shifts the spiritual atmosphere around you. It declares your trust in a God who is bigger than your enemy. It opens doors that fear and despair lock shut.

When you choose gratitude in the middle of lack, you are not being naive. You are being strategic. You are fighting with one of the most powerful weapons in the spiritual arsenal.

## DECLARATIONS

- **I choose gratitude as a discipline, not as a feeling.**
- **I will forget not all of God's benefits toward me.**
- **Every good thing in my life is evidence that God is already providing for me.**
- **My testimony of what God has done builds faith for what He will do.**
- **Gratitude shifts the atmosphere. I am a grateful person.**
- **I will not let the noise of lack drown out the music of grace.**

CHAPTER FIVE

# Something Is Always in Your Hand

*"Then the LORD said to him, 'What is that in your hand?' 'A staff,' he replied."* — **Exodus 4:2**

Moses was standing at a burning bush, having just been handed the most audacious assignment in human history. He was to walk into the most powerful empire on earth, demand the release of millions of enslaved people, and lead them to a promised land he had never seen.

His response was essentially: Are you sure you've got the right guy? I don't have anything to offer.

And God's response is one of the most disarming things in all of Scripture. He didn't argue with Moses' resume. He didn't produce a list of qualifications Moses didn't know he had. He simply asked: What is that in your hand?

A staff. A shepherd's walking stick. The most ordinary, unremarkable tool in the ancient Near East.

Later, in the hands of Moses — surrendered to God — that simple stick would be used to part the Red Sea.

## The Lie of "Not Enough"

One of the most paralyzing aspects of a poverty mindset is the belief that you have nothing to work with. I'm talking about the belief that before you can take a step forward, you first need something you don't have. More money. More education. More connections. A better starting point.

What if that belief is a lie?

What if the question God is asking you right now is the same one He asked Moses: What is that in your hand?

Not what do you wish you had. Not what do other people have that you don't. No. What do you have? Right now. In this moment. In this season.

You have something. I am confident of it. It may seem small. It may seem ordinary. It may seem completely inadequate for the size of the problem you face. But so did a shepherd's staff. So did a widow's last handful of flour. So did a boy's five loaves and two small fish.

God has a history of doing impossible things with inadequate resources — once they are placed in His hands.

## The Miracle of the Oil

> *"Elisha replied to her, 'How can I help you? Tell me, what do you have in your house?' 'Your servant has nothing there at all,' she said, 'except a small jar of olive oil.'"* **— 2 Kings 4:2**

A widow came to the prophet Elisha with a crisis that sounds achingly familiar. Her husband had died and left her in debt. The creditor was coming to take her sons as payment. She had nothing.

Except for a small jar of olive oil.

Elisha's instructions were strange, perhaps even embarrassing: go borrow empty jars from all your neighbors. As many as you can get. Then go home, shut the door, and start pouring.

She poured. And the oil flowed. It kept flowing — jar after jar after jar — until there were no more containers left. And the moment the last jar was full, the oil stopped.

There is a detail in that story I don't want you to miss: the oil stopped when the jars ran out. The limit on the miracle was not God's supply. It was the number of containers she collected.

What you bring to God limits what He can multiply.

She brought what she had. She obeyed in the face of impossibility. And the supernatural met her at the intersection of her obedience and her lack.

## What's in Your Hand?

Let me ask you, seriously and practically: What is in your hand right now?

Maybe it's a skill you've been using for others but haven't thought of as a source of income. Maybe it's a relationship, a network, a reputation for reliability. Maybe it's a creative gift you've been ignoring because it doesn't feel "practical." Maybe it's a small amount of time that you could redirect toward something generative. Maybe it's knowledge — hard-won from years of experience — that someone else needs and would pay for.

Maybe it's simpler than that. Maybe it's the willingness to show up faithfully in a place where others have quit. Maybe it's a generous spirit. Maybe it's the ability to make people feel welcome and seen. These are resources.

I am not suggesting that every need gets met by some hustle you haven't discovered yet. God is not limited to your entrepreneurial creativity. Sometimes provision comes supernaturally from directions you never anticipated. But the story of Moses and the story of the widow and the story of the boy with the loaves all point in the same direction: start with what you have. Offer it. Surrender it. Watch what God does with it.

Something is always in your hand. Let it be enough to start.

## DECLARATIONS

- **I have something to offer. I am not starting from nothing.**
- **I offer what I have to God, and He multiplies what I surrender.**
- **The miracle is at the intersection of my obedience and my lack.**
- **I will not wait until I have more. I will start with what I have.**

- **God is not intimidated by the smallness of my beginning.**
- **What seems ordinary in my hands can become extraordinary in God's.**

CHAPTER SIX

# Speak to Your Mountain

> *"Truly I tell you, if anyone says to this mountain, 'Go, throw yourself into the sea,' and does not doubt in their heart but believes that what they say will happen, it will be done for them."* — **Mark 11:23**

Jesus said something that is either the most liberating truth in human experience or the most reckless claim ever made, depending on what you believe about the man who said it.

He said you can speak to a mountain.

And the mountain will move.

The mountain. Whatever immovable, impossible, looming thing stands between you and the life God has for you.

You can speak to it. And it will move.

## The Creative Power of Words

This is not a new idea. It is woven into the very first page of Scripture. God created the universe by speaking. He said "Let there be light" — and light appeared. He spoke, and matter obeyed. He spoke, and order came out of chaos.

And then He made you in His image.

The implication is stunning: human beings, made in the image of a speaking God, carry within them a capacity for creative, directional speech. Our words are not just sounds. They are seeds. They create atmosphere. They shape the environment around us.

Proverbs 18:21 says it plainly: "The tongue has the power of life and death." Not just emotionally or psychologically. There's something more to this. There is a power in speech that operates in the spirit realm in ways we are still only beginning to understand.

This is why the way you talk about your financial situation matters — not just for your mood, but for your future.

## The Language of Lack vs. The Language of Faith

When I say "the language of lack," I mean the kind of talk that confirms and entrenches a poverty mindset. Things like:

*"We can't afford it. We never have money. Everything always costs more than we expect. Things are never going to change."*

These statements may feel honest. They may even be factually accurate descriptions of your current situation. But they are planting seeds. And those seeds grow into the future you are speaking.

The language of faith is not dishonesty. It is not denying reality. It is speaking to your mountain rather than about it.

There is a crucial difference between these two postures:

*Speaking about your mountain: "This debt is enormous. I will never get out from under it."*

*Speaking to your mountain: "Debt, your days in my life are numbered. I am a debt-free person in the making."*

One speaks from the position of the mountain's victim. The other speaks from the authority of a child of God who carries the "creative" power of the Kingdom in their words.

## You Are a Prophet of Your Own Life

I want to give you a frame for viewing this truth: you are prophesying your own future every time you speak.

This is serious. Think about what you said about your financial situation in the last twenty-four hours. What did you say to your spouse, your friend, yourself? What did you mutter under your breath when you checked your account balance? What story did you tell about your life?

You are not just describing your reality. You are creating it.

This is why declarations are not just feel-good affirmations. They are acts of spiritual warfare. They are the sound of someone refusing to agree with the enemy's narrative and choosing instead to agree with what God has said.

When you declare "I am more than a conqueror," you are not lying. You are agreeing with Romans 8:37.

When you declare "My God shall supply all my need," you are not pretending. You are agreeing with Philippians 4:19.

When you declare "I am the head and not the tail," you are not being arrogant. You are agreeing with Deuteronomy 28:13.

You are agreeing with God. And when you agree with God, things move.

## The Practice

Start today. Pick one specific mountain — one specific financial obstacle, one specific area of lack — and begin to speak to it.

Not about it. To it.

Declare what God has said about that area. Speak it out loud, daily, with as much faith as you can muster — even if it's small. Even if it feels awkward. Even if your circumstances laugh at you.

Circumstances always change more slowly than declarations. But they do change.

Keep speaking. The mountain is listening. And mountains have to obey the children of God.

There is also a practical dimension here. When a declaration becomes a mindset, it starts quietly reshaping your decisions, your habits, and your expectations — often below the level of conscious thought. You begin to move differently. And movement changes everything.

## DECLARATIONS

- **I speak to my mountains. They do not speak to me.**
- **My words are seeds, and I am planting seeds of abundance.**
- **I am a prophet of my own future, and I am prophesying good things.**
- **I agree with what God has said, not with what my circumstances say.**
- **My God shall supply all my need according to His riches in glory.**
- **I am the head and not the tail, above and not beneath.**

CHAPTER SEVEN

# The Culture You Are Creating

*"Where there is no vision, the people perish."* — **Proverbs 29:18, KJV**

Every home has a culture.

Not every family has explicitly thought about that culture, or intentionally shaped it — but it exists. It is the invisible atmosphere inside your four walls, the unspoken beliefs and assumptions that govern how everyone in your household thinks, speaks, and behaves. It is the stories that get told, the conversations that happen at the dinner table, the way people talk about money and the future and God and possibility.

And here is the thing about culture: it is not just a description of what is. It is a creator of what will be.

The culture of your home is a prophecy.

If the culture of your home says "we never have enough," the people inside it will tend to live into that story. If the culture of your home says "God provides for us and we are people of generosity and hope," something entirely different takes root.

This is one of the most important things I can tell you: you are not just fighting for your finances. You are fighting for the culture of your home — and through that, the trajectory of the generations that come after you.

## The Generational Dimension

Poverty is often not just a financial condition. It is a culture that passes from generation to generation. The beliefs, the language, the attitudes, the patterns of thinking and behavior — these are inherited just as surely as eye color or height.

But here is the good news: cycles can be broken.

You are not obligated to live the story that was handed to you. You are not required to pass on the culture you received. You have been given, through the Spirit of the living God, the power to become the person who ends the cycle.

Yes, you can be the person in your family line who stood up and said: This stops here. My children will not inherit a poverty mindset from me. I am changing the culture of this family.

That is one of the most courageous things a human being can do. And it starts with you — not with your income, not with your circumstances, but with your beliefs and your choices right now.

## What an Abundance Culture Looks Like

An abundance culture is not a culture of materialism. It is not about having the best things or chasing wealth as the primary goal of life. It is something much richer and much more enduring.

An abundance culture is one where children hear their parents thank God for provision, even when times are hard. They grow up knowing that their family talks to God about needs and trusts Him to respond — and they have seen Him respond.

Generosity is practiced even in seasons of lack. Small acts of generosity — sharing a meal, giving what you have, holding nothing with clenched fists — create a current in the household that runs counter to scarcity. You cannot be genuinely generous and maintain a poverty mindset at the same time. Generosity is the behavior of someone who believes there is enough.

In this culture, people speak about the future with hope. Not naively. Not ignoring real challenges. But with the settled confidence that God is good and that good things are ahead.

Failure is processed as learning, not as confirmation of permanent defeat. The message inside an abundance culture is not "See? This always happens to us." It is "What did we learn? How do we grow? What does God want to do in this?"

The Bible is present and spoken. The stories of God's provision are told and retold. Testimony is currency. Children know the stories of what God has done — in the family, in the church, in Scripture — and those stories become the foundation of their own faith.

## You Are the Culture Maker

I want to say something to you directly: you have more power to change the culture of your home than you realize.

It doesn't require a different income. It doesn't require a windfall or a miracle financial turnaround before you begin. The culture changes when *you* change. When you start saying different things, thinking different thoughts, responding to hardship from a new posture.

Your children — whether they are young or grown — are watching. They are reading the atmosphere you create. They are absorbing the story you tell about God, about life, about possibility.

What story are you telling them? What culture are you creating?

Because that culture is a prophecy. And you get to choose what it prophesies.

## DECLARATIONS

- **I am a culture maker. I am intentionally creating an abundance culture in my home.**
- **The cycle of poverty ends with me. My children will inherit hope, not lack.**
- **I am generous even in seasons of scarcity, because I believe there is enough.**
- **My home is a place where God's provision is celebrated and testified.**
- **I tell stories of God's faithfulness so my family lives in faith, not fear.**

- **I am building a legacy of abundance in belief, even before it shows up in my bank account.**

CHAPTER EIGHT

# Hope Is a Decision

*"Now faith is confidence in what we hope for and assurance about what we do not see."* — **Hebrews 11:1**

I have met people who have had hope crushed so many times that they are afraid to hope again.

Maybe you are one of them.

You have believed before. You have prayed before. You have declared and trusted and waited — and the thing you were hoping for did not come. Or it came, and then it went. Or it came in a form so different from what you expected that you almost missed it. And slowly, quietly, hope became a dangerous thing. Something to protect yourself from.

Because if you don't hope, you can't be disappointed.

I want to speak gently but directly into that place.

"Hope deferred makes the heart sick" — that is Proverbs 13:12, and it is an honest acknowledgment that the pain of unfulfilled hope is real. Scripture does not pretend otherwise. But the verse doesn't end there: "but a longing fulfilled is a tree of life."

There is a tree of life on the other side of the deferred hope. And the only way to reach it is to keep hoping.

## What Hope Actually Is

In our culture, hope has become almost synonymous with wishful thinking. "I hope it doesn't rain." "I hope things work out." A vague, passive, fingers-crossed kind of sentiment.

But biblical hope is something entirely different.

The Greek word used most often for hope in the New Testament does not mean wishful thinking. It means confident expectation. An anticipation grounded in the character and promises of God. Hope, in the biblical sense, is not a feeling you have when circumstances are favorable. It is a choice you make about where you anchor your confidence — regardless of circumstances.

This is why Paul can say that we "rejoice in hope" even while also noting that "suffering produces perseverance; perseverance, character; and character, hope." Hope is born in the furnace of difficulty, not in the comfort of easy circumstances.

Hope is not the absence of pain. It is the presence of confidence in a God who is bigger than the pain.

## Hope as an Anchor

> *"We have this hope as an anchor for the soul, firm and secure."* — **Hebrews 6:19**

An anchor doesn't keep you from experiencing the storm. It keeps you from being moved by it.

The boat still rocks. The waves still come. The wind still howls. But the anchor holds, and you don't drift.

This is what hope does in the life of someone who is walking through financial hardship. It does not make the hardship disappear. It keeps you from being carried away by it. It keeps you from making desperate decisions born out of fear. It keeps you from giving up the day before the breakthrough. It keeps you tethered to the truth that God is working — even when you cannot see it, even when you cannot feel it.

Hope is the anchor. And you get to choose whether to drop it.

## The Enemies of Hope

I want to briefly name the things that attack hope, because knowing your enemy is the first step in defeating it.

*Comparison* is one of the most destructive enemies of hope. When you measure your behind-the-scenes life against someone else's highlight reel, despair is almost inevitable. Other people's apparent abundance can make your own season feel even darker. But you are not living their life. You are living yours. And God is not comparing either.

*Isolation* is another. When we withdraw — from community, from the Body of Christ, from relationships — we lose the voices that remind us of what is true. Hopeless thinking thrives in isolation. We need each other. We need people around us who will speak truth when we can't hear it ourselves.

*Unforgiveness* is a third. It is hard to hope for a good future when you are carrying the weight of bitterness toward people who hurt you. Forgiveness is not just a spiritual obligation — it is a practical necessity for anyone who wants to move forward. It is hard to make progress when you're weighed down by unforgiveness. Release the debt. Not for their sake. For yours.

### A Daily Choice

Every morning when you wake up, before the news reaches you, before you check your balance, before the weight of the day descends — you have a moment. A window.

In that window, you get to decide: today, I will hope. Today, I will anchor myself to the truth that God is good and that He is working on my behalf. Today, I will not be crushed by what I cannot see. Today, I will believe that this is not the end of the story.

That decision, made consistently, morning after morning, creates a new kind of person.

It creates someone who is a dangerous threat to attitudes of desperation and despair. Make that decision today.

## DECLARATIONS

- **Hope is my decision, not my feeling. I choose it today.**
- **I am anchored to the truth that God is working — even when I cannot see it.**

- My hope is confident expectation, not wishful thinking.
- I refuse to let comparison, isolation, or bitterness steal my hope.
- This is not the end of my story. The best chapters are still ahead.
- Every morning I choose: today I will hope. Today I will believe.

CHAPTER NINE

# The God of the Turnaround

> *"See, I am doing a new thing! Now it springs up; do you not perceive it? I am making a way in the wilderness and streams in the wasteland."* — **Isaiah 43:19**

There is a category of miracle in Scripture that fascinates me: the turnaround.

Not the slow, steady progress miracle. Not the gradual improvement miracle. The turnaround — the moment when everything pivots, when the tide reverses, when what looked like certain defeat becomes sudden, stunning, overwhelming victory.

The Bible is full of them.

Esther — a Jewish orphan in a foreign land — walks into the throne room and saves an entire nation from genocide. Turnaround.

The Prodigal Son is eating pig food in a foreign country and then his father runs to meet him on the road. Turnaround.

Lazarus is four days dead, and then he walks out of the tomb trying to motion for someone to unwind him. Turnaround.

Ruth goes from widowed immigrant with nothing to the great-grandmother of King David and an ancestor of the Messiah. Turnaround.

God specializes in turnarounds.

## The Wilderness Way

What Isaiah 43:19 reveals is something about God's method: He makes a way in the wilderness. Streams in the wasteland. The provision comes through the very place that seemed most barren, most hopeless, most devoid of any possibility.

This is important. Your wilderness is not a detour from God's purpose. It may be the very path God is using to get you where He's taking you.

Joseph's path to the palace ran through the pit and the prison. David's path to the throne ran through the wilderness and the cave. Moses' path to the Exodus ran through forty years of obscurity tending sheep.

The wilderness is not the enemy. The wilderness is often the classroom. But it is not the destination. There is always — always — a way through.

## When the Turnaround Comes

Job 42:10 says that the LORD restored Job's fortunes when Job prayed for his friends. Think about that timing. The turnaround came not when Job had everything figured out, not when he had performed perfectly or understood everything God was doing, not when the answers arrived. The turnaround came in the context of prayer and relationship. It came when Job turned outward — toward others, toward God — rather than inward.

I don't want to reduce that story to a formula, because God is not formulaic. But I want to point out that the turnaround always has a context. And in Scripture, that context almost always includes continued trust in God even when understanding hasn't arrived yet.

You may not understand why you are in the season you are in. That's okay. You are not required to understand in order to receive the turnaround. You are invited to trust.

## The Suddenness of God

One of the things that catches people off guard about divine provision is how suddenly it can come.

The people of Israel were at the edge of the Red Sea with Pharaoh's army behind them — and then they were on the other side. Through one night and one morning, the sea parted. Overnight, everything changed.

The early church was praying for Peter's release from prison — and then Peter was knocking on their door. It happened so suddenly that they thought it was a ghost.

God can change a situation overnight. He can shift a trajectory in a moment. He can open a door that was bolted shut yesterday.

I am not telling you that your breakthrough is definitely coming tomorrow. I don't know the specific timeline of your story — only God does. But I am telling you this: do not give up the day before it happens. Do not throw away your confidence the night before the Red Sea parts. Your suddenness may be closer than you think.

## What to Do While You Wait

Wait actively, not passively. Keep showing up. Keep doing the next right thing. Keep serving, keep giving, keep declaring, keep believing. Waiting on God is not passive resignation — it is active, expectant faith. It is a posture that says: I am ready. I am positioned. I am available. Lord, do what only You can do.

And meanwhile, practice saying out loud — even before the evidence arrives — "My turnaround is coming. I serve the God of the turnaround. He is already making a way."

Keep saying it. It is true.

## DECLARATIONS

- **My God specializes in turnarounds. My turnaround is coming.**
- **The wilderness is not my destination. There is always a way through.**
- **I will not give up the day before my breakthrough.**
- **God can change my situation overnight. I will not limit Him with my timelines.**
- **I wait on God actively — with faith, expectation, and readiness.**
- **He is already making a way where I see no way.**

CHAPTER TEN

# You Are Built for More

> *"Now to him who is able to do immeasurably more than all we ask or imagine, according to his power that is at work within us."* — **Ephesians 3:20**

I want to talk to you about your capacity.

One of the subtlest lies of a poverty mindset is not just that things will never change, but that even if they did — even if provision came, even if circumstances shifted — you couldn't handle more than what you currently have. The lie says that you are not built for abundance. You wouldn't know what to do with it. You'd just mess it up.

That is a lie from the pit of hell, and I want to dismantle it thoroughly.

## Made for Dominion

The first thing God ever said to humanity was not "survive." It was not "get by" or "manage" or "just try not to make too big a mess of things."

It was: Be fruitful and multiply. Fill the earth and subdue it. Rule.

> *"God blessed them and said to them, 'Be fruitful and increase in number; fill the earth and subdue it. Rule over...'"* — **Genesis 1:28**

This is your original mandate. Fruitfulness. Multiplication. Dominion. You were designed by God not for bare survival but for fruitful, expansive, world-blessing life.

Sin disrupted that original design — but it did not erase the blueprint. The Gospel is the story of God restoring you to the original design. Not just getting you into heaven, but restoring you to the kind of full, fruitful, purposeful life you were built for from the beginning.

You are not built for poverty. Poverty is not your design. It is a deviation from it.

## The Power That's Already Inside You

Paul's prayer in Ephesians 3 is one of the most audacious passages in all of Scripture. He prays that believers would be strengthened "with power through his Spirit in your inner being" —

and then declares that God is able to do immeasurably more than all we ask or imagine.

That power — the power of the Spirit of the risen Christ — is not something that's coming *someday*. It is not waiting in heaven for the right conditions to be met. It is at work within us right now. In the middle of the hard season. In the middle of the scarcity. In the middle of the questions and the fear and the not-knowing.

The same power that raised Jesus from the dead is available to you today. That is a power that has never met a problem it couldn't solve. That is a power that has never encountered a situation beyond its reach. That is the power that is "at work within us."

You carry the Spirit of the living God. You are not limited to what your natural circumstances can produce. You have access to a supernatural supply line. You are built for more than your current season suggests.

## The Stewardship Invitation

Here is a reframe that has helped many people: what if abundance is not primarily about what you receive, but about what you get to give?

The most flourishing people in the Kingdom are not those who have accumulated the most —

they are those who have become the most generous conduits of God's blessing. They have learned to hold resources with open hands, to receive freely and give freely, to see themselves not as accumulators but as stewards of a Father who owns everything.

When you begin to see wealth through the lens of stewardship rather than ownership, something changes in your relationship to money entirely. You stop being afraid of it. You stop being greedy about it. You start partnering with God around it.

This is the posture of someone built for more: not "how much can I get?" but "how much can I steward well? How much can I be trusted with? How much can flow through me to bless others?"

God is looking for people He can trust with more. Start building that trust now, in the small things, in the season of less. Because the one who is faithful in small things will be given more to steward.

## You Are Not Too Late

I want to speak specifically to those of you who feel like you've run out of time. Maybe you're approaching retirement with nothing saved. Maybe you feel like the window for a better financial life has already closed. Maybe the years have slipped by in survival mode and the thought of "more" feels not just impossible but almost cruel to even hope for.

You are not too late.

God is not restricted by your timeline. He is not handicapped by the years you spent in survival mode or the opportunities you missed or the decisions you made in ignorance or fear. He is the God who redeems time. And He is the God who, as Joel 2:25 promises, can restore the years that the locusts have eaten.

Your story is not finished. You are not too old, too broken, too far behind, or too far gone. You are exactly where you are — and God is meeting you exactly here. And He is good at making up for lost ground and lost time.

## DECLARATIONS

- **I am built for more. Abundance is aligned with my original design.**
- **The power of the risen Christ is at work within me — right now.**
- **I am a steward, not an accumulator. I am trusted with what flows through my hands.**

- I am not too late. God redeems time. He restores years. He restores what my enemy devours.
- God is looking for someone He can trust with more, and I am that person.
- My best days are ahead. My story is not finished.

CONCLUSION

# From Lack to Overflow — A New Story Begins

> *"The thief comes only to steal and kill and destroy; I have come that they may have life, and have it to the full."*
> **— John 10:10**

We have covered a lot of ground together. And I want to take a moment, before you close this book, to sit with what has happened.

Yes, something has happened.

Maybe you can feel it, and maybe you can't yet. Maybe there is a new warmth of hope somewhere inside you, or maybe it's just a seed — small, barely visible, tucked into soil that has been hard for a long time. Either way, something has been planted. And seeds grow.

Let me remind you of what you now know:

You are not what your bank account says. Your identity is rooted in who God says you are — a beloved child, a planned-for person, someone God knew before you were born.

You serve Jehovah Jireh, the God who sees ahead and who provides. The ram is already in the thicket. The provision already exists. You haven't seen it yet, but God has.

Your mindset is your most important asset. The transformation you need begins in the invisible realm of your thoughts, and you have been given the Spirit of God to help you renew your mind.

Gratitude is a weapon and a gift. It trains your eyes to see what is already present, and it shifts the atmosphere in ways that open doors.

Something is always in your hand. You are not starting from nothing. God has a history of doing extraordinary things with ordinary resources that are surrendered to Him.

Your words create your world. Speak to your mountains. Agree with God, not with your circumstances. You are a prophet of your own future, and you are choosing to prophesy abundance.

You are a culture maker. The atmosphere in your home is changing — and it is changing because you are changing. The legacy you leave your children will be one of faith and hope, not fear and lack.

Hope is a decision. You make it every morning. You drop the anchor into the bedrock of God's goodness and refuse to drift, no matter how hard the storm blows.

Your turnaround is coming. God specializes in turnarounds. He makes streams in wastelands and ways in wildernesses. Your sudden turnaround may be closer than you think.

You are built for more. The power of the risen Christ is at work within you. Your story is not finished. You are not too late. God redeems time.

✦ ✦ ✦

## What Happens Next

I want to give you a few simple invitations as you close this book.

First, make the declarations your own. Read them out loud — all of them — every morning for thirty days. Write the ones that hit you most deeply on index cards and put them where you'll see them. Read them until they stop feeling awkward and start feeling true. Because they are true. It just takes time for our minds and hearts to catch up with what God has already declared.

Second, build your testimony record. Start a simple journal — even a few lines a day — of where you see God's provision showing up. Note the small things. The unexpected things. The answered prayers. The moments of grace. Build the record. You will need it on the hard days.

Third, find your community. The journey from lack to abundance is not meant to be walked alone. Find people around you who believe what you aspire to believe, who will speak life over you when you're struggling to speak it yourself, who will celebrate your breakthroughs and stand with you in your setbacks.

Fourth, be generous. Even now. Even in the season of less. Give something. Not out of compulsion but out of the growing conviction that you serve a God who owns everything and who loves to work through the hands of His people. Generosity breaks the power of scarcity-thinking more effectively than almost anything else.

And finally: keep going. Keep believing. Keep declaring. Keep hoping. Keep showing up, one day at a time. He is the God who sees you.

## The New Story

Even while reading this short book, you have begun to write a new story.

Not just a story about having more money — though I believe that is coming. A story about being a different kind of person. A person whose inner world has been renovated by the Word of God and the power of the Spirit. A person who carries an atmosphere of abundance even in seasons of lack. A person who creates a culture that changes the trajectory of generations.

That person is you. Not someday. Now. You already carry this reality. It is in you. It is growing.

The culture of lack is behind you. The culture of abundance is ahead. And the journey from one to the other begins not when the money comes — it begins in your heart, in your beliefs, in your declarations, in the choices you make today about who you are and who your God is.

He is Jehovah Jireh. He sees you. He is not finished. And neither are you.

Go live the new story. He's already in it with you.

# Master Declaration List

*Read these aloud daily — and watch your world change.*

## Who I Am

- **I am not defined by my bank account. I am defined by whose I am.**
- **I am a child of the God who owns everything.**
- **My current season is not my permanent identity.**
- **I am built for abundance — it is aligned with my original design.**
- **I am not too late. God redeems time and restores years.**
- **My best days are ahead. My story is not finished.**

## What My God Is Like

- **My God is Jehovah Jireh — the One who sees ahead and provides.**

- He will meet all my needs according to the riches of His glory.
- The provision already exists. I just haven't seen it yet.
- God is not scrambling. He has already arranged for my breakthrough.
- His supply line never runs out.
- My God specializes in turnarounds. My turnaround is coming.

## How I Think

- I choose to think from the economy of the Kingdom, not scarcity.
- What God has said about me is more true than what circumstances say.
- I am not a victim of my past. I am choosing new thoughts today.
- Breakthrough is normal for someone who belongs to Jehovah Jireh.
- I wait on God actively — with faith, expectation, and readiness.

## How I Speak

- I speak to my mountains. They do not speak to me.

- My words are seeds, and I am planting seeds of abundance.
- I agree with what God has said, not what circumstances say.
- I am the head and not the tail, above and not beneath.
- He is making a way where I see no way.

## How I Live

- I choose gratitude as a discipline, not just a feeling.
- I will forget not all of God's benefits toward me.
- I offer what I have to God, and He multiplies what I surrender.
- I am a steward, not an accumulator.
- I am generous even in seasons of scarcity. There is enough.
- I am a culture maker — building a legacy of faith and hope.
- Hope is my decision. I choose it today. Every day.

# About the Author

J. Randolph Turpin, Jr. is a pastor, author, educator, and podcaster whose ministry spans decades of local church leadership, theological education, and Spirit-empowered teaching. He serves as a mentor for doctoral students at Global Awakening Theological Seminary and hosts the podcast "5 A.M. with Dr. Randy Turpin " — a platform built on the conviction that dawn always follows darkness, and that God has something to say to people in transition.

Randy writes and speaks at the intersection of biblical truth, practical faith, and prophetic encouragement. His work is marked by a deep love for Scripture, an unwavering belief in God's goodness, and a particular heart for the person who feels stuck, overlooked, or behind.

He and his wife Kerry live in Nashville, Tennessee.

www.ingramcontent.com/pod-product-compliance
Lightning Source LLC
LaVergne TN
LVHW010841120826
845149LV00020B/3419

* 9 7 9 8 9 8 9 1 2 5 7 5 3 *